E.CON the ICON

Also by Dr. Eddie M. Connor, Jr.

Purposefully Prepared to Persevere

Collections of Reflections, Volumes 1-3:
Symphonies of Strength

Unwrap The Gift In You

Heal Your Heart

My Brother's Keeper

E.CON the ICON

from Pop Culture to President Barack Obama

Dr. Eddie M. Connor, Jr.

E.CON the ICON. Copyright © 2009, 2015. All rights reserved. Printed in the United States of America. No part of this book, may be reproduced or transmitted in any form or by any means, electronic or mechanical, including photocopying, recording, or by an information storage and retrieval system, without permission in writing from the author. For information, address Norbrook Publishing, 29488 Woodward Ave. Suite 215, Royal Oak, MI 48073

E.CON the ICON and other books by Dr. Eddie M. Connor, Jr. may be purchased in bulk for educational, business, or sales promotional use. For information, please e-mail the Administrative and Markets Department at info@EddieConnor.com.

First edition published in 2009
Second edition published in 2015 by Norbrook Publishing

All scripture references are from the King James Version, New King James Version, and New International Version Bible.

Library of Congress Cataloging-in-Publication Data has been applied for.

ISBN: 978-0-9970504-3-1

10 9 8 7 6 5 4 3 2

This book is dedicated to dreamers, doers, thinkers, achievers, trailblazers, leaders, those who push against the grain of society's pull, the talented, the gifted, the lifted, the incited, the excited! I'm so delighted! So here is my scribe to YOU and YOU will find quotes, that are inscribed to YOU.

Be an innovator. Be an originator. Be iconic. Be educated. Be elevated. Be expressive. Be refreshed. Be revived. Be reinvigorated. Be renewed. Be greater. Be blessed. Be inspired. Be an icon.

- *E.CON the ICON*

CONTENTS

Introduction: Iconic	1
E.CON the ICON - pt. I	
Haters Are My Elevators	6
From Devastation to Inspiration	12
E.CON the ICON - pt. II	
Success Is in Your mind	18
Transforming Tears to Trophies	29
E.CON the ICON - pt. III	
Tragedy to Triumph	36
Situation, Revelation, Manifestation	42
E.CON the ICON - pt. IV	
Lyrical Licorice	54
RIP off the ROOF	62
E.CON the ICON - pt. V	
Educate, Elevate	71
Segregation, Discrimination, Inauguration	79
From Recession to Progression	85
E.CON the ICON - pt. VI	
Glow in the Dark	92
L.O.L (Life of Legacy)	101
E.CON the ICON - pt. VII	
See it...Seize it	109
ICON...I CAN	118
About the Author	129

E.CON the ICON

from Pop Culture to President Barack Obama

FOR MORE ON
E.CON THE ICON

VISIT:
WWW.EDDIECONNOR.COM

INTRODUCTION

Iconic

From time to time, music artists will release a greatest hits album, which includes their top songs. However, as an author, I have composed a collection of my greatest quotes that I'm assured will inspire and motivate you, to latch a hold to any dream or goal that you seek to attain.

These are my greatest linguistic hits in book form! Some are musically intertwined, some have rhythm and rhyme, but it's nothing short of the top of the line. It's not ironic that these quotes are iconic. I inhale and exhale inspiration, it's what I bleed, it's what I believe, it's how I lead! This book is a literary soundtrack for people's lives.

In our world today, the media is so quick to anoint an individual as an icon because of what they possess or what they do, rather than for who they are. Haven't you heard it go like this? He's a great basketball player so he deserves the title. Her fashion is impeccable, look at those Prada pumps, she's iconic. This one's a great athlete, entertainer, musician, etc. However, when will it go like this? What a great leader in the community. He/she is an inspiration to so many underprivileged youth. This teacher expands the parameters of students minds everyday in the classroom. He is not only a great preacher, but an even greater person. Her volunteer work with the homeless sets an example for giving back to those less fortunate.

More than just a Dad, he is a faithful Father. A true icon as a Mother who raised two children to be positive contributors to society. Those aforementioned statements my friend are truly iconic indeed. There is a paradigm shift, permeating our world and I believe this shift redefines what it means to be an icon. What is your definition of an icon?

True admirable icons:

Mothers
Faithful Fathers
Overcomers of Obstacles
Mentors
Cancer Survivors
Soldiers/War Veterans
Missionaries
Entrepreneurs
Hurricane Katrina Surviors and Volunteers
September 11th, 2001 Survivors and Volunteers
Victims who are now Victors
Critical thinkers who critique our world
Inventors
Community Organizers
Philanthropists
Astronauts
Grandmothers and Grandfathers
Holocaust Survivors
Jesus Christ
Africans who survived the middle passage, slavery, etc.
Freedom fighters for justice
Civil Rights Movement contributors
Dreamers (Dr. Martin Luther King, Jr.)
The 44th President of the United States of America
(President Barack Obama)
Teachers who educate and elevate students
YOU
I too am an icon

E.CON THE ICON - DR. EDDIE M. CONNOR, JR.

Connect with me, via www.EddieConnor.com and Facebook, Instagram, and Twitter: **@EddieConnorJr** (social media handle). Be sure to use the hashtag, **#EconTheIcon.**

E.CON THE ICON - DR. EDDIE M. CONNOR, JR.

Haters Are My Elevators

I feel the beat down low, in my feet my soul. You can't defeat my soul!
I'm inspired, I'm bold!

If you can't recognize the good things in yourself, then don't expect for others to see the good things in you.

Even at my worst, I'm first.

Whatever talent or gift that you have been blessed with, maximize your potential and become influential.

Never minimize who you are, for anyone or anything.

Surround yourself with people that build you up, rather than break you down.

A true friend expresses love through and through and is never the hater.

(Proverbs 17:17)

If you want to be a sharp individual, you must sculpt the blade of your life. Surround yourself with individuals who are on the path of purpose. Not those who are intimidated by who you are, but seek to inject wisdom into your spirit, rather than eject the passion from your soul.

You must have a captivating message, in order to eradicate the mess of this age.

Come hell or high water, I'm unstoppable! My dreams you're NOT able to stop.

From Devastation to Inspiration

My words will inspire, to the point that I perspire.

Sometimes the toll to pay for our dreams, must be traversed through the thorny roads of loneliness.

You don't have to worry or hurry, just remain steadfast and sturdy.

You don't have to possess the nobility, to have the ability.

Check the pulse of your life, revive yourself, and activate the power within.

People always get over what they do to others, quicker than what's done to them.

Oftentimes, the greatest pain can be transformed into the greatest potency of power and peace.

Even though you're in a negative situation, you must not capitulate to the negative situation. Rather, you must remain positive in the negative situation through the fortitude of your mind.

Life is all about transforming stumbling blocks into stepping stones.

Every disappointment is an appointment, that pushes you towards the next dimension of your life.

Success Is in Your Mind

Success is in my mind, success is in my hands. So I will think success, I will speak success, because I am successful. I am not a failure. I am a success, because I was born to be the best and nothing less.

I'm so visual,

I even talk in pictures.

See your goal
and seize the goal.

We must allow the Word of God to captivate our minds, whereby we can capture the greatness that often slips through our hands.

While America's kids are at Disney, China's kids are in a dictionary.

Success is often plastered in platinum, baptized in barbecue sauce. It looks good and it smells good. The word *success* has lines drawn vertically over the letters *S* and diagonally over the letters *C* to where we think success is only about dollars and cents. The terminology is twisted, because you can't make true sense of the word *success* if it's only about what you have. The bigger picture is about who you are and what you contribute to the lives of others.

Forget all the hocus pocus, focus focus.

Your true definition is more vivid, than high definition.

Life is not only about being successful, but it's about being significant.

You can matriculate from the ghetto and achieve greatness.

You can maneuver from the suburbs and become a success.

How do you rehabilitate the black psyche that has been demoralized, demonized, and debilitated by the shackles of society?

The road to success is often a lonely road, yet in that experience of loneliness, God expresses His lovingkindness.

The fruit of our actions, is connected to the root of our thoughts.

Release the power in your mind and forge ahead to your mission.

Situational setbacks, are only setups for success.

You can't be successful, if you're not teachable. Keep learning and growing.

You literally are the substratum of your thoughts. You are spirit, soul, and mind. In essence these are matters of the mind, because it's your mind that matters.

True success is not about what you possess, or who you can impress.

Move the energy of your mind towards your mission, because it's too powerful for the past to hold it. Your mission is too enormous, for an individual to control it. Your mission is too hot for a hater to hold it.

Don't settle for it, if God didn't promise it. Greater is on the next level!

Transforming Tears to Trophies

You can move from opposition, to an elevated position.

Whenever you refuse to express the gift that you are, you then repress who you are.

Your ebullience and energy will propel you

from hurt to healing, from depression to distinction, from breakdown to breakthrough, from pain to power, from destitute to destined, and from carelessness to carefulness.

The character of a champion is cultivated in the chaotic and cataclysmic circumstances of life. I wonder do you *C* it?

When will you move from life's opposition, to the right position?

You can think positive in negative situations.

Rejection is direction. NO is New Opportunity

Energize the weak, mend the broken hearts, bring deliverance to the captives, restore sight to the spiritually blind, bring liberty to the bruised, bring hope to the hopeless, enrich the poor, bring direction to the destitute, and provide guidance to the fatherless. (Luke 4:18)

In these times of life, when storms arise amid the lakes of luxuries, without a single warning and sweep over our boats of benevolence, our hands must reside and abide as a haven of harmony and our love must be shed abroad, like a lyrical lullaby.

God's favor on you, isn't determined by people's opinions of you!

3 words:

Know. Your. Worth.

Tragedy To Triumph

I don't just have testimony, but **I am** a testimony.

You cannot have power, over what you permit.

Stop worrying about what you left behind…focus on what's coming ahead!

Sometimes God ADDS to your life….by SUBTRACTING people from it!

The darkest hour of your struggle, can become the brightest hour of your victory.

In order to traverse to a greater level in life, we need to come out of some things and some things need to come out of us.

There is a method to life's madness, found in the joy of God's gladness.

Don't just GO through… GROW through, to get to your goal.

Your greatest exhibition of strength, occurs at your weakest moments of despair.

You are a symbol of freedom, so enlighten the world with your gifts and talents. Discover and unlock your purpose. Inspire, esteem, motivate, cultivate, enumerate, liberate, invigorate, regenerate, imbibe tranquility to bring about unity, reconciliation, determination, and steadfast love to revive our nation.

Situation, Revelation, Manifestation

You had to go through the process of the pit and endure the pain of the prison, in order to elevate to the promise of the palace.

God has given us the internal resources of His word, to overcome the external circumstances in the world.

You are not an accident. You are not an incident. Your life has purpose according to God's providence.

Christmas is not about our presents, but it's about recognizing God's presence in our lives.

It's not about the presents under the tree, but it's about Christ who hung on the tree.

When God starts removing things, it's because He's positioning you for better things!

Stop settling for what's convenient. Wait to receive what's consistent.

Your giving determines your living.

Between the preparation and the manifestation, for your destination…there is God's demonstration.

Do you have the network? The Father, Son and Holy Spirit. Not Verizon, but your breakthrough that's on the horizon.

God has to call us out to call us to. He has to bring us out, to bring us to. (Matthew 22:14)

Jesus was born in the boroughs of Bethlehem, grew up in the ghettos of Galilee, nestled in the neighborhoods of Nazareth, and died for **YOU**…so that **YOU** can live for Him.

Only the Christ of the cross, can bring you out of circumstance and crisis.

The accoutrements of this world are constructed to satisfy our physical body, yet oftentimes our spirit is malnourished. Why be robust and voluptuous on the outside, yet anorexic and anemic on the inside?

When God favors you… people who don't like you, can't do anything about it!

God is able to give us interior resources, in order to confront the exterior trials and difficulties of life.

Rather than looking past the cross we must look to Christ, for through Him we can reclaim our lives.

Somebody's praying for what you're complaining about. Count your blessings, not your problems.

Sometimes we have to turn off CNN, BET, and MTV, in order to hear from G-O-D.

Every negative situation is an expression for true revelation, elevation, and ultimate manifestation for your declaration of power.

You are enough, the right person will recognize your value and worth!

For too long, we have allowed people to whisper **sweet nothings** in our ears and that's what it has materialized to, nothing. Rather, we should allow God to whisper **sweet somethings** in our ears, so that our lives can become something greater than before.

Lyrical Licorice

You might possess the model physique, but that doesn't mean you pass the role model critique.

Some people have a filet mignon appetite, but a filet-o-fish attitude.

You might have a Louis Vuitton account, but is your life accountable to the path of positive progression?

It's not what you wear, it's how you wear it. Originate your swagger. Strut your style.

You'll drive yourself crazy, trying to figure out how God's going to work it out…breathe and believe!

Your life is defined, by what you think about yourself…not what others think about you.

True peace doesn't derive from what you drive… True peace illuminates power, passion, perseverance, and purpose. (Isaiah 26:3)

How can you give thanks, if you don't live thanks? How can you give thankfully, if you don't live thankfully?

My words are literary design. Fashionably, my words tailor your mind.

Do more than look to receive a blessing…look to be a blessing!

2 UNHAPPY people… cannot make a HAPPY relationship.

Cast **ALL** of your cares on God, because He has the healing tissues, for your hurting issues.

(I Peter 5:7)

When you become a person of love, you will attract it…you won't have to chase it!

Stay true to becoming the best, that you can be… love yourself, know your worth and invest in it!

There are some people, that you have to love from a distance. If they're not helping you grow…let them go!

RIP

off

the

ROOF

Too many people would rather R.I.P., than RIP the ROOF off their dreams.

Avoid detours to destruction. Rather, journey the avenues of acclimation and the boulevards of benevolence.

Your impending fear, can lead to your greatest discovery.

Some people have a degree in **Me-ology** because everything about them, their narcissistic desires, and viewpoints.

If your vision is blurry… you'll never see the opportunity.

Operate in your lane. Use your gift. Don't replicate or duplicate, originate.

You'll get to the next level…if you don't settle.

In order for us to be what we ought to be, we must forsake the ways of that which we used to be.

The greatness of what we ought to be, resides in the mentality of you and me.

You'll ruin it, if you rush it. Pause, pray, and be patient.

Step out from among the crowd and exhibit greatness.

You're too extraordinary, to be ordinary. You are distinct and distinguished. You are the epitome of God's creation. You will be lifted because you are gifted.

In order to soar to the stratosphere of stability, your mind must be locked into the vision of your mission. For the vision of your mission, is immersed in your position.

You can't tell your dreams, to everybody!

You must believe, in order to achieve. You've got to exude passion in order to persevere. For your strength must be made perfect, it must be released in times of weakness.
(II Corinthians 12:9)

Stop trying to fit...where you don't belong.

You possess the internal fortitude to fight. So resurrect faith in the face of fear. Resurrect determination in the midst of doubt. Resurrect positive thinking in a negative environment. Resurrect a smile in the midst of sadness. Resurrect the optimism of overcoming the odds.

Educate, Elevate

It's either education or incarceration.

Education or incarceration is not necessarily physical. Rather, this is an incarceration of the mind and spirit. Locking you out of opportunity. Some people are in a prison without bars.

Impact minds in today's perilous times.

Be a critical thinker, in chaotic times.

Knowledge must be disseminated from your house, to the White House.

Our brothers must realize that their ability, is not predicated upon their street credibility. You don't have to do four years in a prison house, when you can do four years at Morehouse.

Education must provide the proper interpretation and life application.

Our generation must be uplifted and empowered, to be change agents…in their communities, schools, universities, churches, careers, lives, and the lives of others.

America's educators must discover innovative methods and mediums to captivate the minds of youth, that will engage them to the point of discovering nuggets of knowledge in books.

Learn your history, it's a bridge between the past and your destiny.

Share your story. Educate and use it as a testimony.

What if the spelling for *education,* became *edYOUcation?* Young learners must begin to understand that their future progression ultimately depends upon themselves. **YOU** must apply yourself and the lives of those around **YOU!**

You may not have attended Harvard, Princeton, Yale…but you did graduate with a **'Life Lessons Degree'** from the **School of Hard Knocks** and the **University of Adversity**.

Find strength through adversity…impact your community and university!

Segregation, Discrimination, Inauguration

The mere fact of President Barack Obama's meteoric rise to prominence, exemplifies the notion that young men don't have to relegate themselves to being a playa, pimp, or drug pusher, when one can be President.

President Barack Obama's historic Presidency must not be seen as a monument, it must be the beginning of a new movement.

Racism is not over and full equality, is not a true reality. There are still battles to fight.

In order for America to change, the people of America must change. America has uprooted herself, from the tree of truth and the foundation of faith.

How do you rehabilitate the black psyche, that has been debilitated by the shackles of society?

The fate of the world's progression does not rest on the shoulders of one person, but all people as a collective construct of our communities.

Our world revels in the grandeur and magnanimity of the new camelot, with President Barack Obama assuming the White House. Yet, we must never accept the trade off that 4 years (or more) of a black Presidency, eradicates 400 years of slavery and oppression in America.

In a world that privileges those, who have the most money…we must express care, for the least of these.

From Recession To Progression

Young Jeezy raps about economic recession, but Jesus speaks about your eternal progression.

(John 10:10)

God desires that we make intercession, for our life progression.

(Romans 8:26)

Your value is not in what you have, but your value is in who you are.

You can have quantity and not have quality. You can have good fortune, without having a huge fortune.

Never settle for being a product of your

environment, rather be a productive asset to your environment.

Challenge and channel your gifts within, in order to pursue a positive means for greatness.

We must not allow possessions to validate us, only our purpose on this planet validates our value.

You can have everything and still have nothing, you can have a lot of things and still have nothing.

No financial recession will not hinder your progression, God has got you covered.

God's favor, is greater than man's money.

The tragedy of September 11th, put us all on the same scale. Whether we have 50 million or 50 cents, a Benz or a Beetle, Prada or nada, it doesn't mean anything. Our lives are our most valuable possessions.

Your life is the true value of you…love yourself!

If you don't recognize your value in your life, then you won't recognize the value of life.

A true Queen knows how to pray for you, encourage you, and nurture the KING in you!

Glow In The Dark

Exude a distinct and distinguished aura, that is uncanny.

You are NOT the NEXT generation, you are the NOW generation.
(I Peter 2:9)

Be your authentic self… be YOUnique

Our young ladies need to realize, they don't have to shake it like a salt shaker, or pepper shaker for that matter. Rather, she must allow God to shake her, mold her, make her, and take her to where He has called her to be.

Your body is more valuable, than being labeled as a vixen…you have a mind that has a viable vision.

Shine and show the world your light within. Without a shadow of a doubt, you were born to win.

You are a Statue of Liberty. Uphold truth and light up the world.

Don't allow yourself to be distracted and take detours to destruction, when you can advance via the avenues of acclimation.

In the various sectors and streams of society, there is an ardent call to shed light on the disenchanted and debilitating conundrums of life. The call of character, creativity, and ingenuity seek to transform the mundane lifestyle, into a masterful litany of excellence.

The call of character and commitment, echoes from the ghettos to the government, from caves to castles, from every human ability to the achievers grandeur and nobility.

When one door closes, two open…expect double!

You have the inner strength that will stand the storms of abuse and calm the rains of mistreatment. Your inner power will get you to it and God's grace, will guide you through it.

Our very boroughs and boulevards are crying out for an exhibition of excellence, that will reach into the very abyss of one's soul and resurrect power to prevail. Revitalize the faith, that eradicates fear and imbue the passion, that will overcome every distraction.

Treat your relationships like CLOTHES…make sure they're TAILOR made to fit your life!

L.O.L

Life

of

Legacy

Life is not only about living luxuriously, but it's about leaving a legacy… through the life, that you live.

God has so fixed it that people may not ever read a Bible, but they will read your life.

True love is not reactive. True love is proactive.

Love yourself and know your worth…if they don't recognize it, that's their loss.

Don't stop being GOOD…because somebody treated you BAD!

The relationship will never be RIGHT…with the WRONG one!

Real love hangs in there with you…it doesn't leave you hanging!

Real love will protect you…not neglect you.

A PRETTY face means nothing…if you have an UGLY attitude!

You have been assigned a work to complet…don't waste your time, trying to compete with others.

You're too unique…to compete.

Evaluate your temporary pleasures, versus your permanent treasures.

Don't do permanent things with temporary people.

Let go of people, who refuse to let go of the past.

Understand that your hands are a haven of hope. Your words are a lyrical lullaby. Your mind is the splendiferous conduit, by which all obstacles will be conquered.

The question to be answered is will you take a stand, or will you allow someone to stand on you?

God's word is the outlet and you are the plug. When you plug into the outlet of His word and flip the switch of faith…He will illuminate the darkness in your life. For "His word is a lamp unto my feet and a light onto my pathway."

(Psalm 119:105)

See it, Seize it

See your goal and seize the goal.

Blast past your past, create your future, dictate your future!

Every breath is a blessing…inhale peace, exhale purpose!

The way you view yourself, will transform the perception of your circumstance.

You are capable, you have the capability. Now just take the cap off your ability.

Make sure they value who you are…not what you have.

You can't love anybody properly, until you first love yourself adequately.

God is doing it, so nobody else can take credit for it!

The plan for your life…is greater than the pain, that you've experienced in life.

You must have 20/20 vision for your future.

You must repeat to yourself, that you are valuable. You are a man of might. You are a lady of liberty, and you are the epitome of excellence.

Spiritually see it and naturally seize it.

Your words create your world. Your confession dictates your possession.

Your work earns no applause, if your effort is a lost cause.

Do it for a cause, not for applause.

You are what you say and you will have, what you say.

Time is of the essence and this is the time to expand the parameters of your mind. Approach every obstacle with dogmatic determination, as a stimulus to reach the apex of opportunity.

(Ecclesiastes 3:1-8)

Many individuals are worried about the provision, for their vision. If you write the vision, God will appropriate the provision for our mission.

(Habakkuk 2:2)

Work your vision, God will give you provision.

ICON...
I CAN

Delete the letter **T** from the words **I can't** and transform it into **I CAN**.

(Philippians 4:13)

You can matriculate from the ghetto and achieve greatness. You can maneuver from the suburbs and become a success. You can do something good in your neighborhood

Your life's mission is so magnanimous that it will vanquish death, your mission will propel you beyond the haters, movers, and shakers.

The words **"I can"** are denoted twice in the title, **African American...** affirming the notion that **WE CAN** do twice more, than what we ever imagined.

The very best of you and me, resides in our inspired destiny.

The very definition of your life's purpose, must compel and propel you to persevere.

It's not what you have that makes you valuable. It is the strength of who you are that makes you invaluable.

The strength of your aspirations, dreams, goals, and mission is immersed in your conviction.

You've must press beyond the stress and believe that your outcome will be blessed.

This is your time to shine. This is your season of reason. This is your day to convey. This is your minute to win it. This is your moment to own it. This is your instance to be iconic. This is your year to cheer and celebrate God's blessings.

How will you move towards the destiny of your future…if you only live presently, in your past?

God is opening doors… you never knew existed!

Hard work will take you…where talent can't keep you!

It's okay to want better for yourself…don't let anybody stunt your growth!

Chase purpose not money, and money will chase you!

Think **BIGGER** than your bank account!

Pick up your vision, dream again! Pick up your joy, laugh again! Dry your eyes, wipe your tears, and smile again! This is your day to live, so live again! As long as you've got life and believe, then you can achieve! Maintain your vision and you will succeed.

E.CON THE ICON - DR. EDDIE M. CONNOR, JR.

ABOUT THE AUTHOR

DR. EDDIE M. CONNOR, JR. is a resident of Detroit, Michigan and grew up in Kingston, Jamaica. He is an Author, College Professor, International Speaker, Minister, and Founder of the *Boys 2 Books* literacy/mentoring program. Dr. Connor empowers people to overcome obstacles and walk in their unique purpose, by sharing his story of overcoming stage four cancer. He has earned a Doctorate and serves as Graduate Education Professor, at the prestigious Marygrove College.

While working alongside, former Congressman Hansen Clarke, Dr. Connor's efforts assisted in developing a Resolution in the 112th U.S. Congress (H.Res.721), to express that bolstering literacy amongst African American and Hispanic males, is an urgent national priority. The development of the resolution, became the impetus for President Barack Obama's, *My Brother's Keeper* initiative.

Dr. Connor has garnered prestigious honors, for his community activism and unique leadership ability, such as the Dr. Martin Luther King, Jr. Humanitarian Award, NAACP Speaker Award, Black Male Engagement Leadership Award, The Spirit of Detroit Award, and named one of the top 100 leaders in *Who's Who in Black Detroit*.

Dr. Connor has been featured via BET, CBS, FOX News, NBC, PBS, TCT, The Steve Harvey TV Show, The Tom Joyner Show, The Word Network, USA Today, and many other media outlets. He was also featured in the acclaimed BET documentary, *It Takes A Village to Raise Detroit*.

Dr. Connor speaks extensively on the subjects of education, leadership, overcoming obstacles, and maximizing your purpose. As an international speaker, much of his work extends throughout Jamaica and South Africa. Dr. Connor empowers people at churches, conferences, community centers, and colleges, by inspiring and motivating others to overcome the odds.

WEBSITE:
Sign-up to receive weekly motivational messages at
www.EddieConnor.com

SPEAKING ENGAGEMENTS/ MEDIA REQUESTS:
info@EddieConnor.com

SOCIAL MEDIA:
(Facebook, Instagram, Twitter)
@EddieConnorJr
#EconTheIcon

www.ingramcontent.com/pod-product-compliance
Lightning Source LLC
Chambersburg PA
CBHW032052150426
43194CB00006B/502